Books should be returned on or before the
last date stamped below

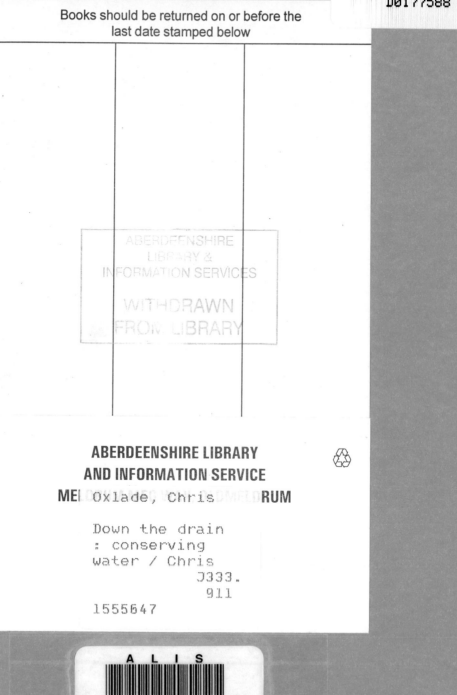

**ABERDEENSHIRE LIBRARY
AND INFORMATION SERVICE**
MEL Oxlade, Chris **RUM**

Down the drain
: conserving
water / Chris
            J333.
               911
1555647

You can Save the Planet

Down the Drain:
Conserving Water

Chris Oxlade and Anita Ganeri

Heinemann
LIBRARY

www.heinemann.co.uk/library
Visit our website to find out more information about Heinemann Library books.

To order:
☎ Phone 44 (0) 1865 888066
▤ Send a fax to 44 (0) 1865 314091
▯ Visit the Heinemann Bookshop at www.heinemann.co.uk/library to browse our catalogue and order online.

First published in Great Britain by Heinemann Library, Halley Court, Jordan Hill, Oxford OX2 8EJ, part of Harcourt Education. Heinemann is a registered trademark of Harcourt Education Ltd.

Oxlade, Chris
Down the drain :
conserving water
/ Chris Oxlade,
J333.
911
1555647

Editorial: Nancy Dick
Design: Richard Park
Illustrations: Q2A and Jeff Edwards
Picture Research: Maria Joannou and Virginia Stroud-Lewis
Production: Camilla Smith

Originated by Dot Gradations Limited
Printed in China by WKT Company Limited

ISBN 0 431 04170 9
09 08 07 06 05
10 9 8 7 6 5 4 3 2 1

British Library Cataloguing in Publication Data
Oxlade, Chris and Ganeri, Anita
Down the Drain: Conserving Water.
– (You Can Save the Planet)
333.9'116
A full catalogue record for this book is available from the British Library.

Acknowledgements
The publishers would like to thank the following for permission to reproduce photographs: Alamy p. **23**; Bridgeman Art Library p. **27**; Corbis p. **9**; Corbis/ Anna Clopet p. **15**; Corbis/Johnny Buzzerio p. **16**; Corbis/Michael S. Yamashita p. **5**; Dk Images p. **18**; Gareth Boden p. **8**; Getty Images/Stone p. **11**; Ginny Stroud-Lewis p. **14**; ICCE/Mark Boulton p. **13**; Impact/Mike McQueen p. **25**; Rex Features p. **7**; Science Photo Library/Colin Cuthbert p. **12**; Science Photo Library/Dr Gopal Murti p. **24**; Science Photo Library/Dr Jeremy Burgess p. **26**; Still Pictures p. **22**; Tudor Photography pp. **4**, **17**, **19**, **20**, **21**.

Cover photograph of a water park, reproduced with permission of Alamy/The Photolibrary Wales.

The publishers would like to thank Nick Lapthorn of the Field Studies Council for his assistance in the preparation of this book.

Contents

Words appearing in the text in bold, **like this**, are explained in the Glossary.

Why do we need water?

Water is vital for our lives. Every plant, animal, and person needs water to grow and stay alive. Water is also an important **resource**. We use it for washing, cleaning, cooking, and drinking. Farmers use it for growing **crops** and raising animals, and factories need it for making things.

Science Behind It: Drinking water

Two-thirds of your body is made of water. You lose water when you breathe out, sweat, and in your urine. To replace all the lost water, you need to drink about 2 litres of water every day. You need more if you are playing sport or are in hot weather. You could stay alive for more than a month without food, but you could only survive for a few days without water.

Water is the most important substance that we need to stay alive.

What is the problem?

Two-thirds of the Earth is covered with water, but most of it is salty. Only one per cent of all the Earth's water is fresh water that we can use. This means that water is a precious resource. Some places are very short of water, so it is important that we do not waste it. Instead we must save, or conserve, it. We must also keep water supplies clean, because dirty water can spread diseases and harm the people and animals that drink it.

4

Taking Action: What can I do?

If we waste too much water, we will have problems finding enough water in the future. You might think that the problem is too big for you to do anything about. But if each of us does something, together we can make a big difference. Look out for Taking Action boxes like this one throughout this book. They will give you ideas for action you can take to conserve water.

Why should we conserve water?

Two-thirds of the Earth is covered in water so you might think that there would be plenty of water to go round. But most of this water is in the seas, and sea water is salty. You cannot drink it because it would make you more thirsty, and sick, too. The salt also means we cannot use sea water for washing, cleaning, or growing plants. So we need to conserve water because there is not much water that is suitable for us to use.

What water can we use?

The water that we can use is called fresh water. It does not contain salt. Only three per cent of all the water on Earth is fresh water. Most of this is locked away as ice near the Poles and in glaciers on high mountains. The only water available for us to use is in rivers and lakes, and under the ground in **aquifers**.

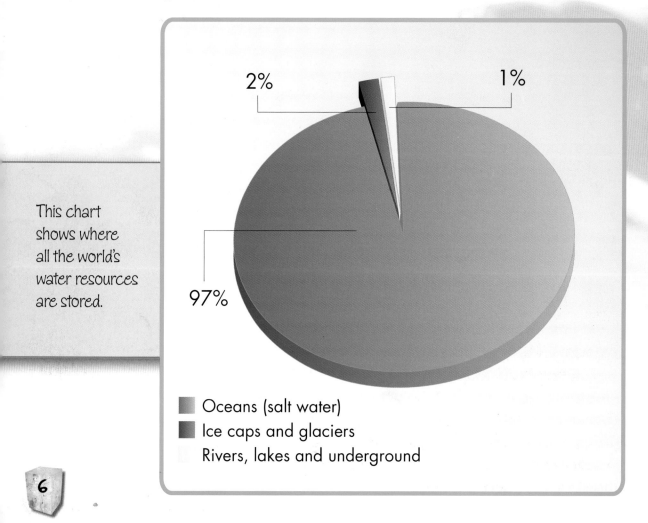

This chart shows where all the world's water resources are stored.

2%

1%

97%

■ Oceans (salt water)
■ Ice caps and glaciers
  Rivers, lakes and underground

What happens if we use too much water?

If some people use more water than they need, other people can be left short of water. For example, if people take too much water from one part of a river, there may not be enough water for people living further downstream. If we take too much water from underground sources, the water may eventually run out. In hot, dry countries, and when there is a drought, conserving water supplies becomes even more important.

These boats used to float in the Aral Sea. Today there is about 75 per cent less water in the sea than in 1960.

Harming the environment

Taking too much water from rivers and lakes can also harm the animals and plants that live there. Taking water changes the natural flow of a river. This can make it difficult for fish and other animals and plants to live in the river. Taking too much water from lakes and **wetlands** can make them shrink, leaving plants that grow around their edges without water.

How much water do we use?

Have you ever thought about how much water you use every day? It is probably a lot more than you think. As well as the water you drink and wash with, water is used at home and school to prepare your food, and to wash your clothes and dirty dishes. Huge amounts of water are used in factories to make the things you buy from the shops.

How much do I use at home?

In a **developed** country, an average person uses anywhere between 100 and 200 litres of water a day indoors at home. That is enough to fill a bath full to the brim. Amazingly, most of this water is used for flushing the toilet. Added to this, you probably use up 25 litres of water every day at school. People in hot, dry places use more water in their gardens.

Water helps keep you clean. It washes dirt from your hands and takes it away down the drain.

Taking Action: Keep a water diary

Work out how much water you use by keeping a water diary. During the day, make a note every time you use some water. Write down what you used the water for and when you used it. If you use a tap, count the number of seconds the tap runs for. Use the figures below to work out the total amount of water you used in the day.

Toilet flush: 10 litres per flush
Running tap: 1 litre every ten seconds
Shower: 30 litres
Bath: 80 litres
Garden hose: 15 litres per minute
Washing machine: 100 litres per cycle

Who else uses water?

Farmers need lots of water for growing **crops**, especially when the weather is hot and dry. It takes more than 50 litres of water to grow just one orange. Factories also use large quantities of water for processing **raw materials**, and making things. For example, it takes between 5 and 10 litres of water to make a newspaper.

We use billions of litres of water every year to help crops grow.

9

Where does our water come from?

The water we use comes from three places. These are rivers, lakes, and rocks under the ground. Your water might come from just one of these places or from all three. Water gets into rivers, lakes, and rocks because of the water cycle. The water we use is on its way round the water cycle.

Science Behind It: The water cycle

The water cycle is the way in which the Earth's water is used over and over again. Without the water cycle, we would have no fresh water. During the water cycle, water **evaporates** from the sea into the **atmosphere**. Only the water evaporates, leaving the salt behind. In the atmosphere, the water **condenses** to form clouds. Water falls from the clouds as rain or snow. Some falls directly into rivers or the sea. Some soaks into the ground or runs off into rivers and flows back to the sea, where the cycle begins again.

The water cycle carries water from sea to land and back again.

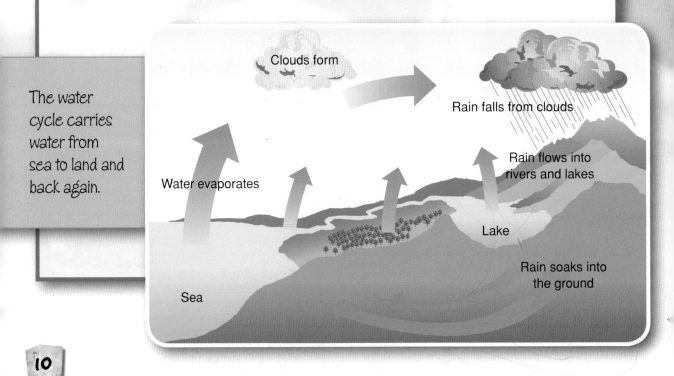

Clouds form

Rain falls from clouds

Water evaporates

Rain flows into rivers and lakes

Lake

Rain soaks into the ground

Sea

What is a reservoir?

A reservoir is an artificial (human-made) lake. Some reservoirs take water from rivers flowing along in deep valleys. A dam is built across the valley to catch the water. Then the water is stored in the reservoir until it is needed. Reservoirs also store water that is pumped out of rivers. Taking water from rivers is called abstraction.

How is water stored underground?

Some rocks have lots of tiny spaces inside them. Water can trickle through these spaces. If the water cannot drain away, it fills the rock with water. Gradually, this builds up an underground store of water. These water-filled rocks are called **aquifers**. We get water out of aquifers through wells drilled down into the rock.

A dam like this can hold enough water for a large town for several months.

How does water get to us?

Water comes to our schools, homes, offices, and factories along pipes under the ground. Water that flows along these pipes is called mains water. A wide pipe carries the water to towns and cities. Then smaller pipes carry the water along each street and to each building. Some buildings have a water tank in the roof to store water in case the mains water is cut off.

Many people in **developed** countries depend on a complex system of underground pipes to bring them water.

Is the water dirty?

Water taken from rivers, reservoirs, and boreholes can be dirty, so it is cleaned before we can use it. To do this, it is pumped to a **water treatment plant**. The water goes through a metal grill to remove any large bits of rubbish. Then chemicals are added to get dirt out and to kill any **micro-organisms** living in the water. Finally, the water is tested to make sure that it is clean enough to drink.

Can we get water from the sea?

It is possible to use water from the sea, but first it must have the salt taken out to make fresh water. This process is called **desalination**. Desalination plants (or factories) are built in places very far from any sources of fresh water. They work by boiling the water, which leaves the salt behind. However, desalination uses up lots of energy. This makes the water very expensive.

Does everybody have mains water?

Millions of people in the world do not have mains water supplies. They cannot just turn on a tap to get their water. Instead, they get water from a well and carry it home in containers. They are very careful not to waste their water.

In many countries, people must get their water from a community well like this one in Mozambique.

What happens to waste water?

What happens to all the dirty water that goes down the drain? What about the water that comes out of washing machines, and that we flush down the toilet? The answer is that is goes back into rivers or the sea. But it is always cleaned first to remove any waste, dirt, and chemicals.

Water from a sink begins its long journey to the water treatment works.

Where is dirty water cleaned?
Waste water flows into underground pipes called drains. It flows along the drains into large pipes, called **sewers**, under the streets. The sewers lead to a **water treatment plant**, where the water is cleaned. The clean water is poured back into a river or flows along pipes out to sea.

How is waste water cleaned?

First, the dirty water is poured through a metal grill, like a sieve. This catches large rubbish, such as twigs and plastic bags. Then the water flows slowly through large tanks, where smaller bits of sand and grit settle to the bottom. **Micro-organisms** are added that eat waste and other harmful micro-organisms. Now the water is clean. The dirt that has been removed from the water forms a sludge. The sludge is buried underground, used as **fertilizer**, or burned.

Water is cleaned by bacteria in these tanks.

Science Behind It: Bacteria cleans your water

Bacteria are tiny micro-organisms. Some bacteria are dangerous because they cause diseases. But some kinds of bacteria and other micro-organisms called protozoa help to clean dirty waste water. They eat waste in the water and any other kinds of bacteria in the water that might cause disease.

Taking Action: Don't pour away chemicals

Some chemicals, such as motor oil, paint, and weed killers, are difficult to remove from water. It is better not to pour them away. Ask your family to store waste chemicals carefully, where they will not get spilled, and not to pour them down the drain. Then ask a parent or teacher to help you find out where they can be disposed of safely.

How can we save water at home?

There are three simple ways of cutting the amount of water we use. First, we can waste less water. Second, we can collect rainwater and use it instead of tap water. Finally, we can reuse some water instead of pouring it away.

Dripping taps should be fitted with a new washer to stop leaks. This can save a lot of water.

How can I waste less water?

Huge amounts of water are just poured down the drain without being used for anything. This is a terrible waste. Here are some simple ways to stop wasting water:

- Don't let the tap run while you are brushing your teeth. Turn it off!
- Fill a basin or sink for washing in, instead of letting the water run.
- When you turn on the hot tap, collect the cold water that comes out first. Use it to water houseplants or the garden.
- Use a dishwasher or washing machine only when you have a full load.

Does water leak away?

Lots of water is wasted because it leaks away through dripping taps or toilet cisterns with worn-out washers. A dripping tap wastes up to 25 litres of water a day! Check your house for dripping taps and overflow pipes, and ask your parents to replace the washers.

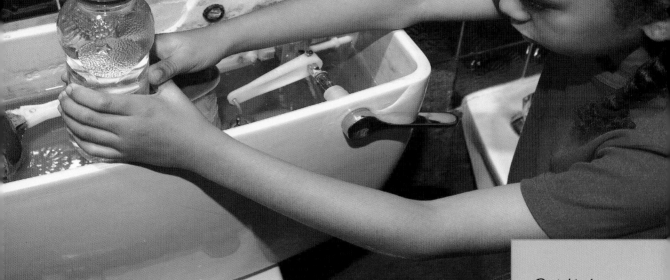

Taking Action: Use water efficiently

Save water by only using as much as you really need. One easy way is to take a quick shower instead of a bath. This could save more than 50 litres of water a day. You can save a litre of water every time you flush the toilet by putting a litre bottle of water in the cistern. When your parents buy a new washing machine or dishwasher, ask them to choose a model that uses water efficiently.

By taking up space in the cistern, a bottle of water reduces the amount of water needed to fill it up again.

How can we save water outdoors?

Think of all the ways we use water outdoors. We water plants and lawns in the summer, and we use water for cleaning windows and cars. Here are some ways in which you can stop wasting so much water:

- Water plants and lawns in the evening to reduce **evaporation**.
- Put wood chippings or straw on flowerbeds to reduce evaporation.
- Cut grass a bit longer than normal. This will stop the earth under the grass from drying out quickly in hot weather.
- Don't use a hose pipe when there are water shortages.
- Wash your car with buckets of water instead of a hose.

Straw covers the soil, helping to stop the soil drying out. This means it needs less watering.

Science Behind It: Evaporating water

Evaporation is the way in which liquid water turns into gas when it heats up. If you water your garden during the warm daytime, the water evaporates quickly. It is better to water the garden in the evening, when it is cooler, so evaporation happens more slowly. Then the water has time to soak into the ground.

How can we use rainwater?

You do not need to use clean mains water for the garden. You can use rainwater to water plants and lawns. The best way to collect rainwater is in a water butt. It is like a large barrel and collects rainwater that flows off your roof.

Where can we reuse water?

Reusing water means using waste water for another job instead of simply pouring it away down the drain. For example, you can water the garden with the waste water from cooking food, from peeling and rinsing vegetables, and from a paddling pool. But do not put soapy water on the garden because it could harm the plants.

A water butt like this can provide all the water your garden needs.

Taking Action: Trap run-off

Run-off is rainwater that flows across the land and into streams and rivers. Run-off from your garden normally flows into drains, but you can trap run-off so that it soaks into the ground instead. Try some of these ideas out at home or at school. Ask permission from a parent or teacher first.

- Replace solid concrete paving stones with gravel. This will let water seep through into the ground.
- Build terraces in sloping flower beds so that water can soak into the soil before it drains away.
- Make a rain garden by digging a dip in the ground. Water will collect in the dip, keeping the ground moist. Plants will grow better here than on dry ground.

How can we save water at school?

At school, you use water for painting and washing, in the toilets, in the gym changing room, and for drinking. Water is also used in the school kitchens, and for watering the garden and playing fields. Saving water is not only good for the environment. It also saves money because your school has to pay for every drop of water it uses. You can save water at school in the same ways as you do at home.

If someone forgets to turn off the tap, a lot of water is wasted. This type of self-closing tap turns off automatically.

How can we use less water?

A simple way to save water at school is to make sure you turn off any taps you use. Leaving them running wastes lots of water. Check that other pupils have turned off the taps, too. You could ask your school about putting in taps that turn off automatically. Your school could also put in toilets that flush automatically after each use. Ask about saving water in the school kitchens. Water used to prepare and cook vegetables could be reused to water your school garden.

Taking Action: Water watch!

Tell other pupils and teachers at your school about the importance of saving water by starting a water-watch **campaign**. Make posters for your campaign telling people about the problems of wasting water and suggesting simple ways for saving it. Make posters for the washrooms to remind pupils to turn off the taps. You could also do a presentation at a school assembly and on the school website.

Get your friends involved and see what you can do to help conserve water at your school!

Rainwater harvesting

Some schools have a **rainwater harvesting** system. It is like a water butt, but more complicated. The system collects water that runs off the roof and stores it in a tank. The water is cleaned and used for flushing toilets and washing hands as well as watering gardens and fields. This saves taking hundreds of litres of water from the mains every day.

Case Study: Rainwater harvesting in Delhi, India

The Shri Ram School is in Delhi, India. The school's main source of water is a well that goes down into an **aquifer**. The water is pumped from underground. The school also gets some mains water from the city's supply. In 2000, the water level in the well was dropping and the school was in danger of running out of water. So the school decided to put in a **rainwater harvesting** system.

In most rainwater harvesting systems, the water is stored in tanks above ground, but the school decided to use a system that would store water in the aquifer. Gutters collect the rainwater that flows off the school's roofs. Pipes carry the water to a large tank. Water from the tank trickles down a deep well into the aquifer under the ground.

The Shri Ram School system has been a great success. It collects millions of litres of rainwater each year, much more than the pupils and staff need. Also, the water level in the aquifer has slowly risen again.

CASE STUDY

These girls are learning about a water system at their school in Bangladesh.

Why is clean water so important?

You probably take a supply of clean water for granted at home or school. You can turn on a tap and clean water comes flowing out. But millions of people in **developing** countries are not as lucky. They do not have clean water supplies. They have to use dirty water for drinking and washing because they have no choice.

Is dirty water dangerous?

If harmful chemicals and **micro-organisms** get into the water supply, it can make the water very dangerous. Waste chemicals from factories can make people blind if they get into the water supply. Micro-organisms such as **bacteria** cause diseases such as **cholera** and **typhoid**. Both of these diseases can kill people. More than five million people die every year from drinking dirty water.

When untreated sewage flows through the street, such as in this village in Kenya, it can spread disease.

Science Behind It: Disease in the water

Even water that looks clean can cause diseases if it contains micro-organisms such as bacteria. These bacteria are so small you can only see them with a microscope. Many sorts of bacteria are harmless. In fact, you have millions of harmless bacteria living in your body. But some bacteria make us ill if they get inside our bodies, because they make poisonous chemicals. Our water supply is tested to make sure it is free of harmful micro-organisms.

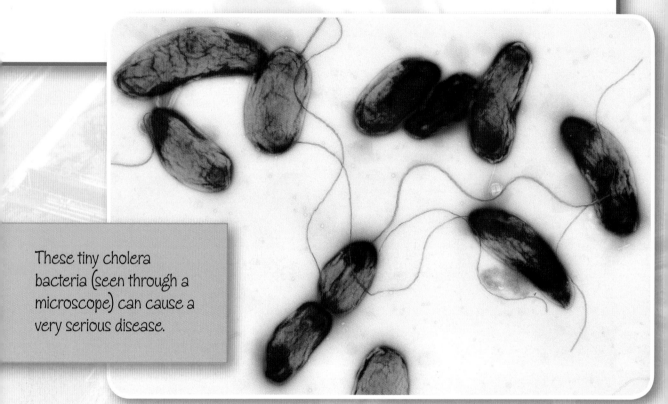

These tiny cholera bacteria (seen through a microscope) can cause a very serious disease.

Taking Action: Collect for charity

Find out about charities that help people in developing countries to have clean water. You could search the internet to find out the names of the charities and what they do. You could donate money from a sponsored walk or swim, or organise a collection at school.

What makes water dirty?

If you are lucky enough to have a supply of clean water, you must take care of it. Having a dirty, **polluted** water supply is as bad as having no water at all. It is very important to keep our precious water supplies as clean as possible. This means that we must not pollute the water in our rivers and **aquifers**. Things that pollute water include human waste, factory chemicals, and farm chemicals. River pollution not only harms people but also animals and plants that live in the river.

Factories are one source of pollution in rivers and streams. This water is called industrial effluent.

Waste water pollution

Sometimes rivers become polluted because waste water flows into them without being cleaned first. The water may contain human waste, chemicals, and litter. In some places, the water is not treated because there is no sewage system and no **water treatment plant**. It flows straight from homes into rivers, lakes, or the sea.

Science Behind It: Plant blooms

Fertilizers, animal waste, and **detergents** contain two chemicals called phosphorus and nitrogen. They are often washed into streams and rivers when it rains. The phosphorus and nitrogen make plants in the river grow very quickly. When the plants die, bacteria start rotting them. Bacteria use up lots of **oxygen** from the water. Then there is less oxygen left for fish and other animals, so they may die.

This water is clogged up with a type of plant called algae.

Taking Action: Pollution watch

Carry out a pollution check on your local stream. Looking at live animals in the water, such as fish, insects, and shrimps, is a good way to check how polluted a stream is. Ask an adult to help you with your study. Use a jar to collect a sample of water. Examine the water with a magnifying glass. If you see many small animals, the water is probably very clean.

Case Study: Cleaning up the River Thames

At one time, the River Thames in London, England, was one of the dirtiest rivers in the world. In the early 1800s, London's population grew to more than a million as people moved into the city from the countryside. There were no water pipes or **sewers**. The people got their water straight from the Thames and put their waste water straight back into the river.

The river became very dirty and by the 1850s, it was like a giant sewer! No animals or plants could live in the water, and the smell was terrible. Many people died from **cholera** because they drank the dirty water.

DIPHTHERIA   SCROFULA   CHOLERA
FATHER THAMES INTRODUCES HIS OFFSPRING TO THE FAIR CITY OF LONDON
(A Design for a Fresco in the New Houses of Parliament.)

This picture shows what people in the 1800s thought of the filthy river.

The Thames became cleaner when sewers were put in, but it was filthy again by the 1960s. Then modern **water treatment plants** were built, and the river began to get cleaner. Fish began to return and in 1974, a salmon was caught in London. It was the first salmon caught there in 140 years! Since then the water has continued to get cleaner.

fact file

- A cubic kilometre is a cube with each side a kilometre long. There are about 1460 million cubic kilometres of water on the Earth. That is 1,460,000,000,000,000,000,000 litres!
- 1,400,000,000,000,000,000,000 litres of the world's water is salty sea water.
- The average person in the USA uses about 200 litres of water per day. The average person in Africa uses about 5 to 10 litres of water per day.
- On average, nearly a tenth of all the water piped to homes is lost because of leaks.
- In Australia between 35 and 50% of all water used at home is used in the garden.
- In the USA more than 550,000,000,000,000 litres of water is taken out of rivers and **aquifers** every year. Much of this is used for watering **crops**.
- About 90% of all the water we take from the mains goes down the drain afterwards. The rest gets drunk or goes on the garden.
- About 40% of the drinking water supply in the USA comes from underground aquifers.
- The High Plains aquifer in North America is 500 kilometres wide and 1150 kilometres long. It contains about 3,680,000,000,000,000 litres of water.
- In your lifetime you will use more than a swimming pool full of water for flushing the toilet.

find out more

Books to read

Earth's Precious Resources: Water, Ian Graham (Heinemann Library, 2004)

Green Files: Thirsty World, Steve Parker (Heinemann Library, 2004)

Websites

There are many useful websites to help you learn more and make plans for taking action of your own.

Water Use It Wisely – learn lots of ways to save water:
www.wateruseitwisely.com

Savewater – Australian site all about saving water:
www.savewater.com.au

United Kingdom Environment Agency – water use and conservation in the UK:
www.environment-agency.gov.uk

Water Aid – charity that helps to bring clean water to people in less developed countries:
www.wateraid.org.uk

Glossary

aquifer layer of underground rocks filled with water

atmosphere layer of air that surrounds the Earth

bacteria tiny living things that live in air, water, or soil

campaign series of things done by a group of people to achieve a result

cholera disease caused by bacteria that infect the intestines

condense turn from gas to liquid

crop plant grown by farmers for food

desalination removal of salt from salt water (for example sea water)

detergent chemical used for cleaning

developed describes a country that has advanced industries and where most people have an education, jobs, a place to live, and food to eat

developing describes a country where many people do not have much money and do not have much education. Such countries often have food shortages, few sources of power, and poor transport systems.

drought long period of time without rain

evaporate turn from liquid to gas, but at a temperature lower than the liquid's boiling point

fertilizer chemical that helps plants grow

micro-organism plant, animal or other living thing that is too small to see with the naked eye

oxygen one of the gases in the air that animals need to breathe to stay alive

pollution something that makes air, water, or other parts of the Earth's environment dirty

rainwater harvesting collecting rainwater so we can use it. This means we take less water from the mains water supply.

raw material material we get from the Earth in its natural state, which we can then use to make other things

resource anything that is useful to people

sewer pipe under the ground that carries dirty water to a water treatment works

terrace area on a slope that has been made level

typhoid disease caused by bacteria that may cause death. Typhoid is spread when people eat food or drink water that has the bacteria in it.

water treatment plant place where dirty water is cleaned before it goes back into rivers or the sea

wetland area of land, such as a marsh or a swamp, that is normally covered with a shallow layer of water

Index

Titles in the *You Can Save The Planet* series include:

Hardback   0 431 04168 7

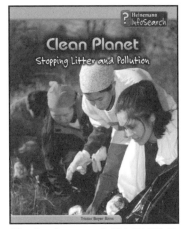

Hardback   0 431 04171 7

Hardback   0 431 04169 5

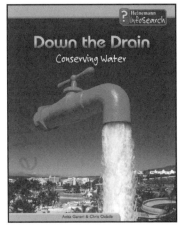

Hardback   0 431 04170 9

Hardback   0 431 04172 5

Find out about other titles from Heinemann Library on our website www.heinemann.co.uk/library